HAL LEONARD
STUDENT
PIANO
LIBRARY

Popular Piano Solos
For All Piano Methods

T0045555

Table of Contents

Book: ISBN 978-0-7935-7722-4
Book/CD: ISBN 978-1-4803-5248-3

HAL•LEONARD®
CORPORATION
7777 W. BLUEMOUND RD. P.O. BOX 13819 MILWAUKEE, WI 53213

Visit Hal Leonard Online at
www.halleonard.com

All My Loving

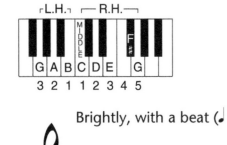

Words and Music by John Lennon
and Paul McCartney
Arranged by Fred Kern

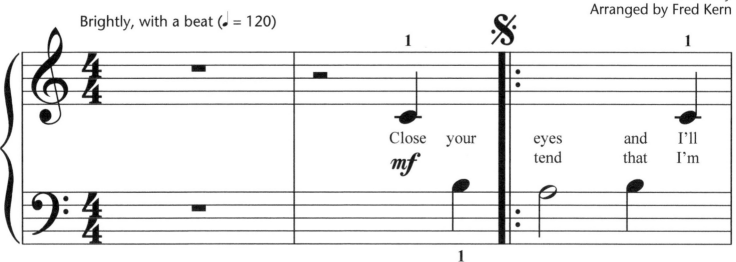

Close your eyes and I'll
tend that I'm

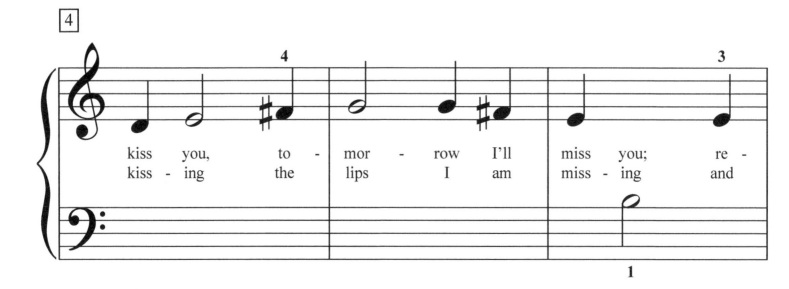

kiss you, to-mor-row I'll miss you; re-
kiss-ing the lips I am miss-ing and

Accompaniment (Student plays one octave higher than written.) 🔘 **TRACKS 1/2**

Brightly, with a beat (♩ = 120)

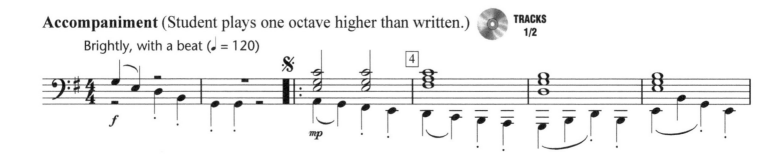

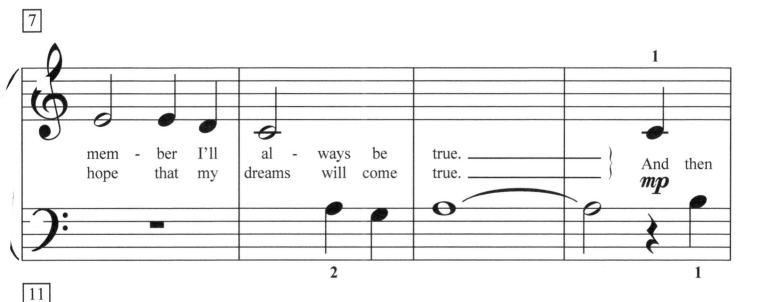

mem - ber I'll / al - ways be / true._____ / And then
hope that my / dreams will come / true._____

mp

while I'm a - / way, I'll write / home ev - 'ry / day,___ and I'll

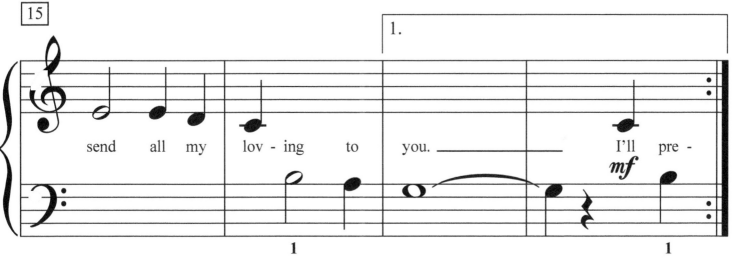

1.

send all my / lov - ing to / you._____ / I'll pre -

mf

p

11

15   1.

mp

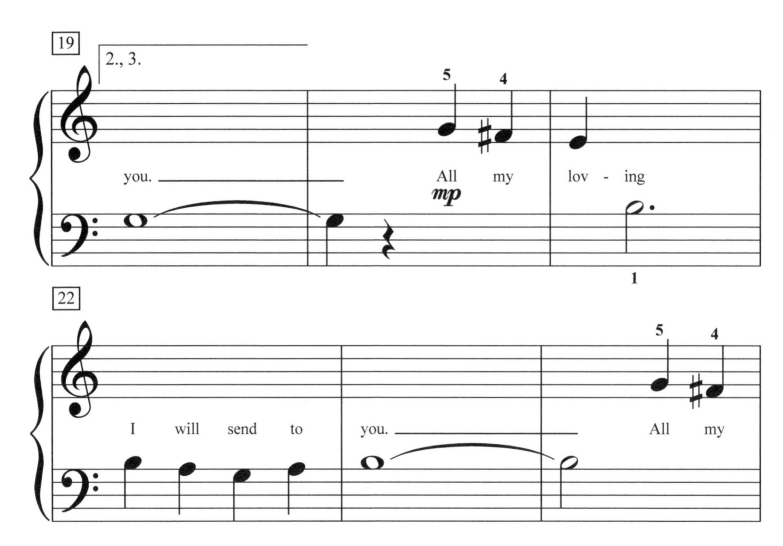

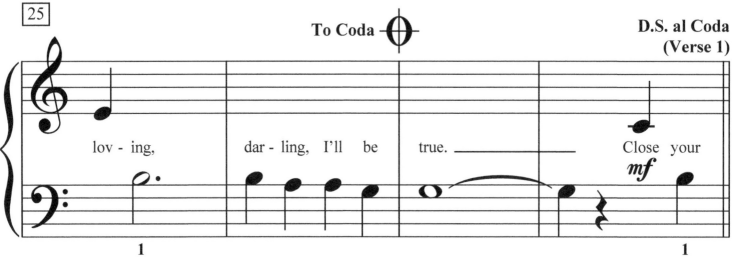

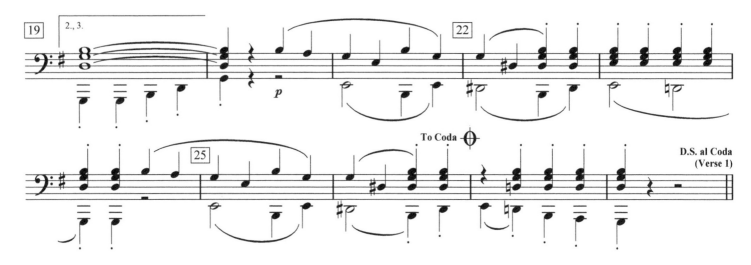

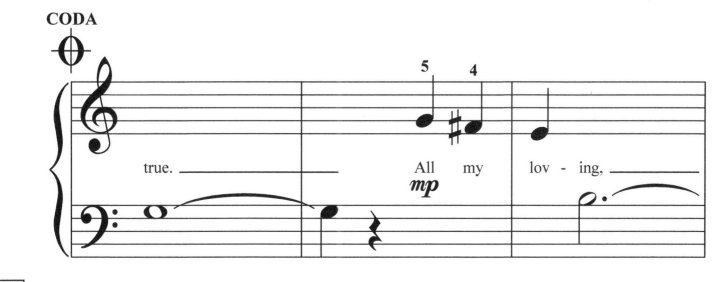

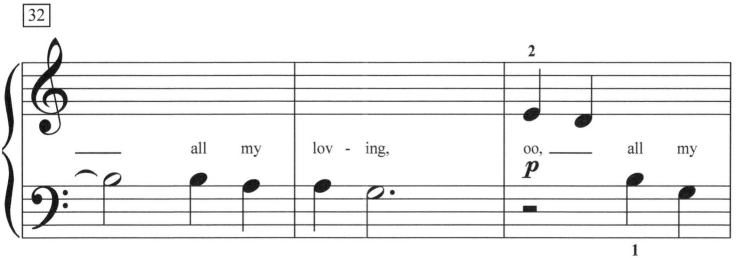

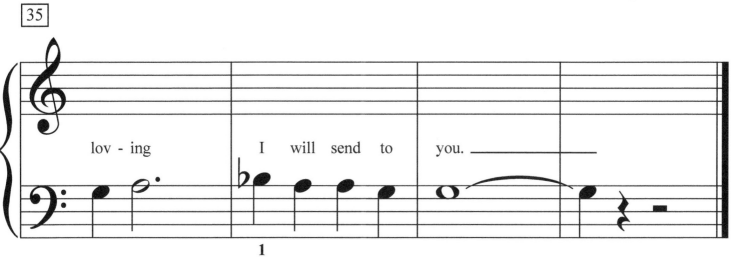

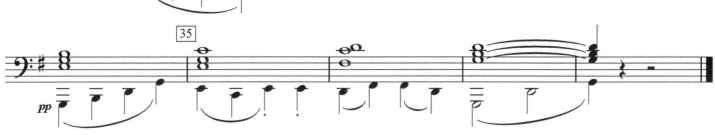

The Bare Necessities
from Walt Disney's THE JUNGLE BOOK

Words and Music by Terry Gilkyson
Arranged by Fred Kern

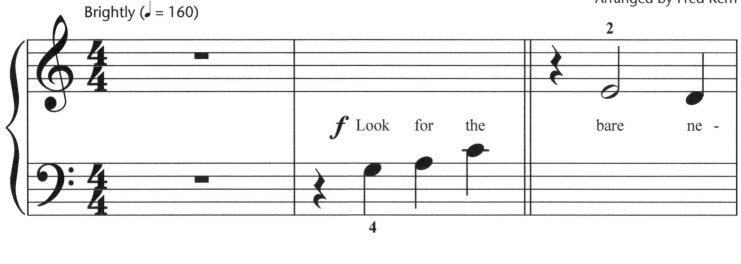

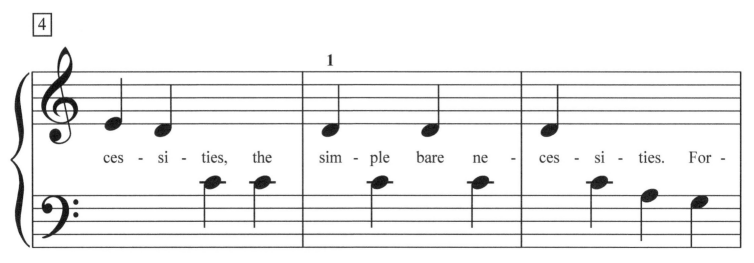

Accompaniment (Student plays one octave higher than written.)

TRACKS
3/4

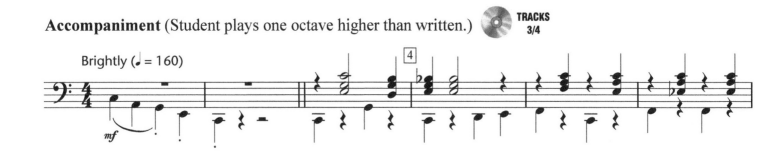

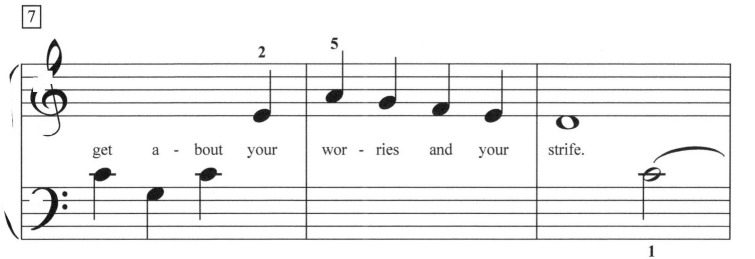

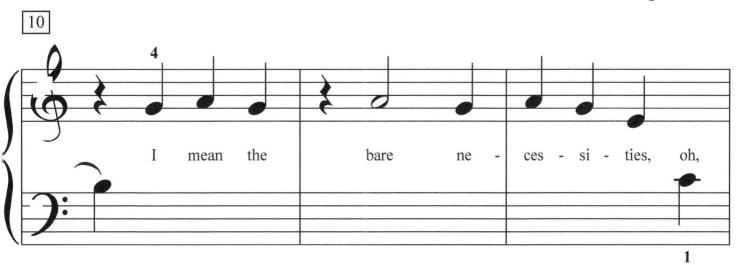

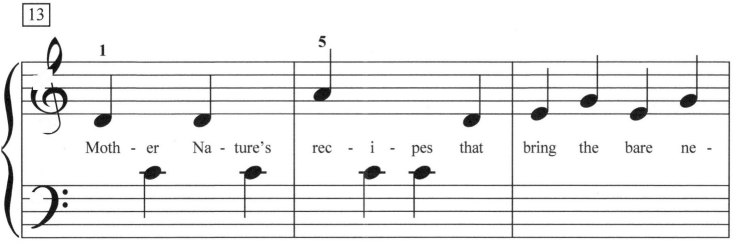

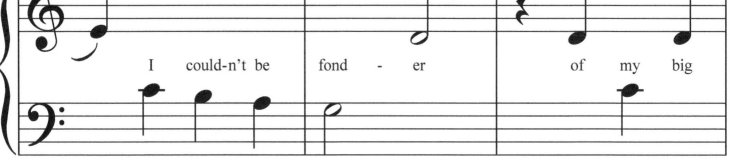

home. The bees are buzz - in' in the tree to make some

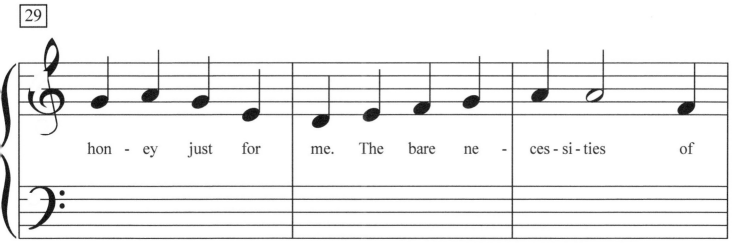

hon - ey just for me. The bare ne - ces - si - ties of

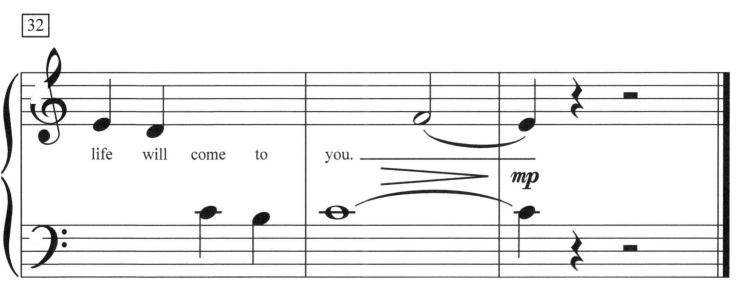

life will come to you. _____ *mp*

Candle on the Water

from Walt Disney's PETE'S DRAGON

Words and Music by Al Kasha
and Joel Hirschhorn
Arranged by Phillip Keveren

Accompaniment (Student plays one octave higher than written.)

TRACKS
5/6

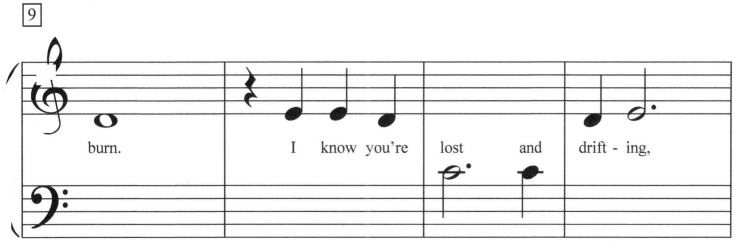

burn.   I   know you're   lost   and   drift - ing,

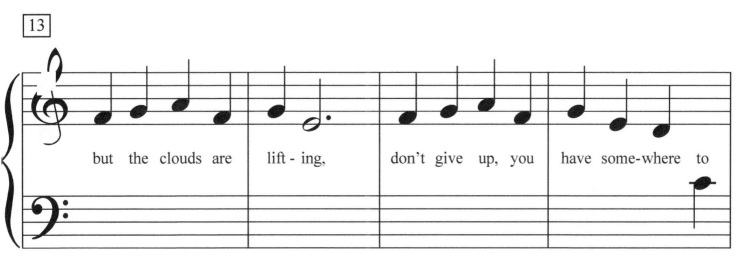

but the clouds are   lift - ing,   don't give up, you   have some-where to

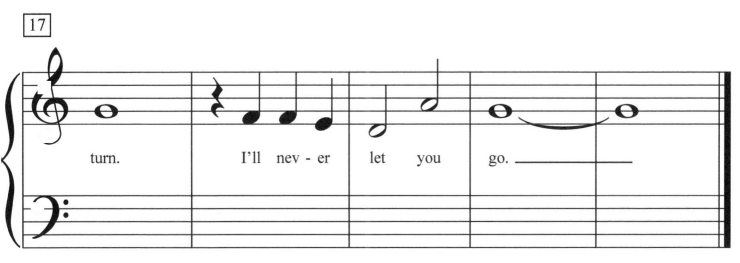

turn.   I'll nev - er   let   you   go. _____

Good Morning

from SINGIN' IN THE RAIN

Words by Arthur Freed
Music by Nacio Herb Brown
Arranged by Mona Rejino

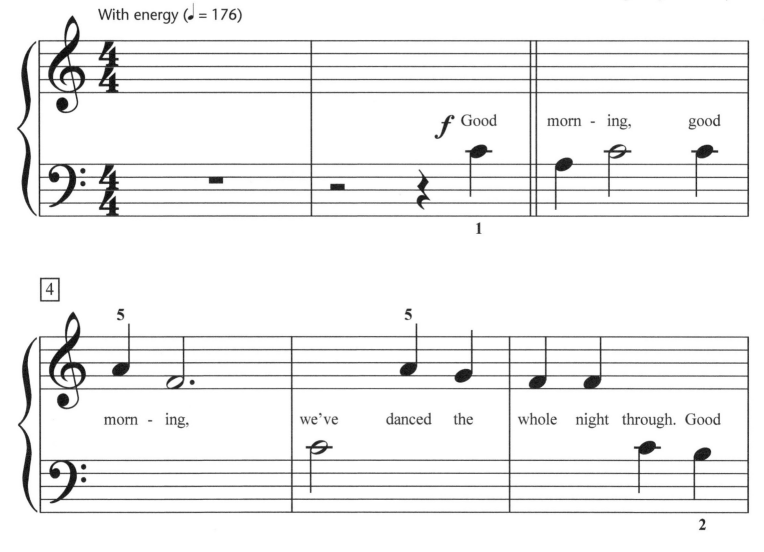

Accompaniment (Student plays one octave higher than written.)

TRACKS 7/8

With energy (♩ = 176)

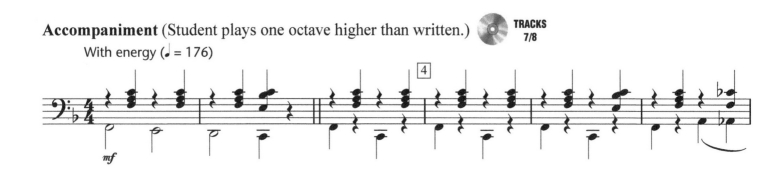

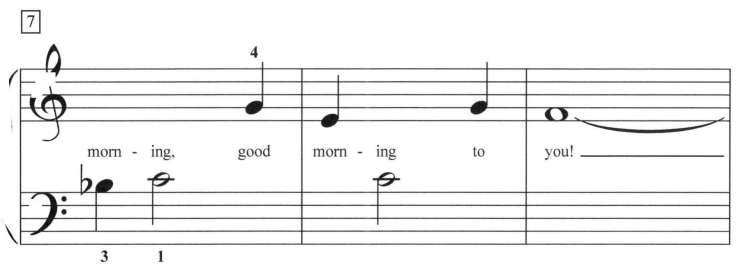

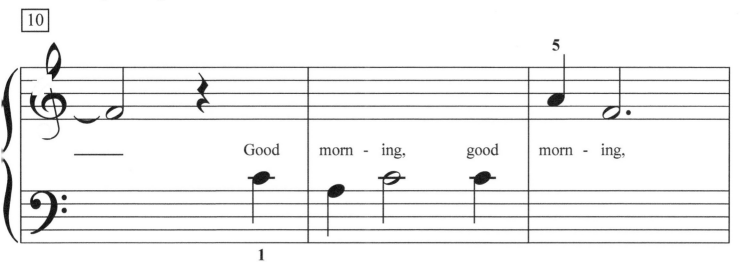

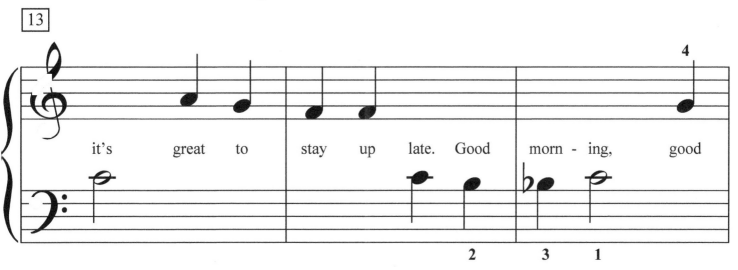

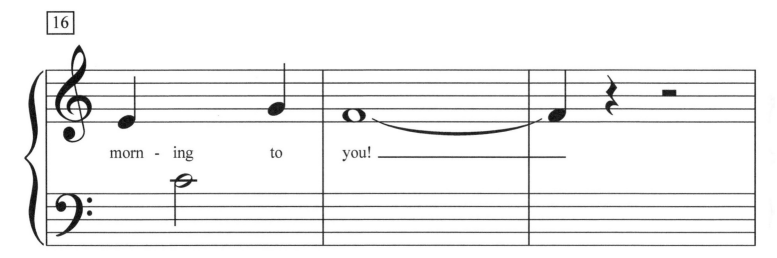

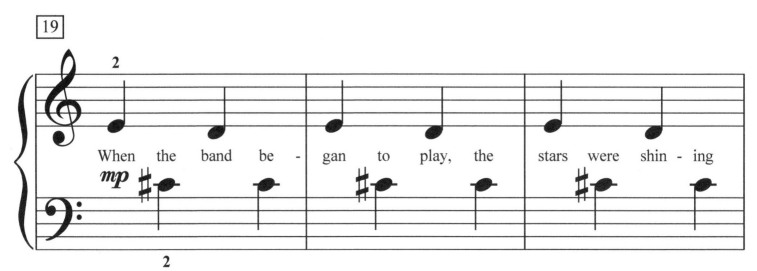

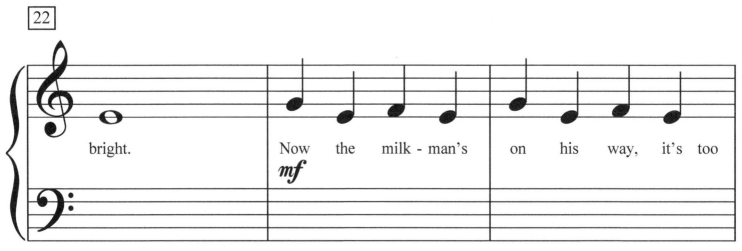

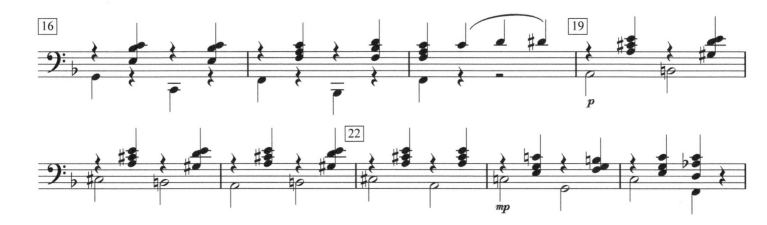

14

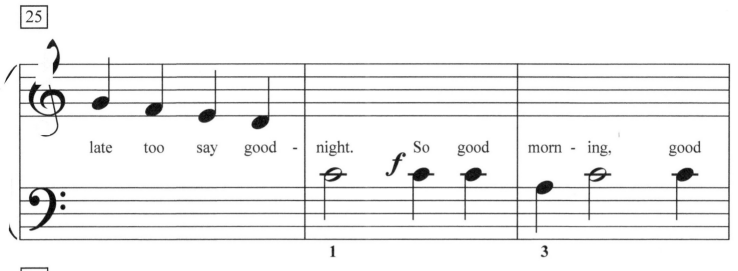

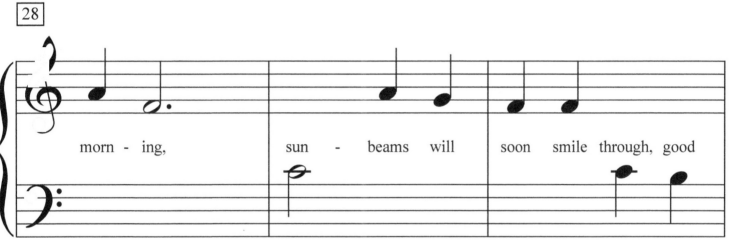

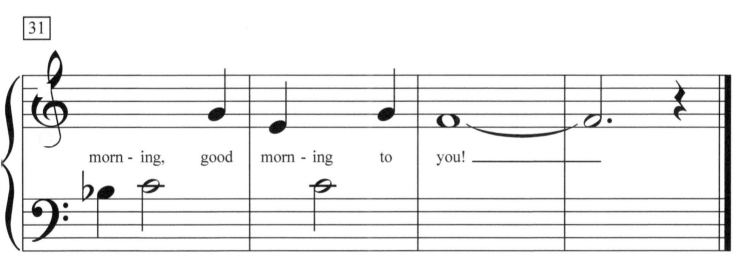

I Just Can't Wait to Be King

from Walt Disney Pictures' THE LION KING

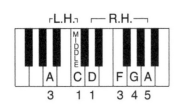

Music by Elton John
Lyrics by Tim Rice
Arranged by Phillip Keveren

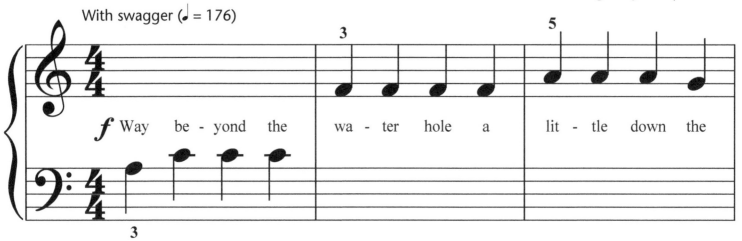

Way be-yond the wa-ter hole a lit-tle down the

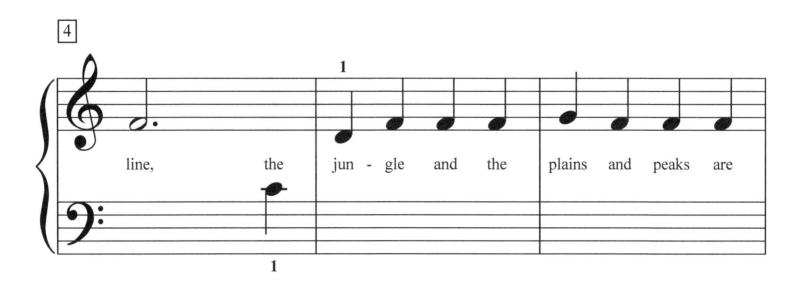

line, the jun-gle and the plains and peaks are

Accompaniment (Student plays one octave higher than written.) TRACKS 9/10

With swagger ($\quad$ = 176)

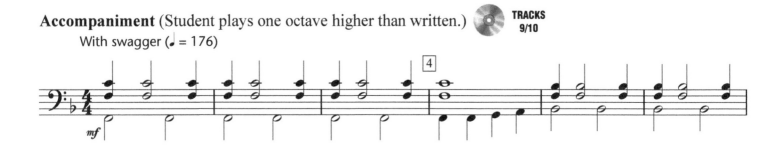

sched - uled to be mine. I'm gon - na be the

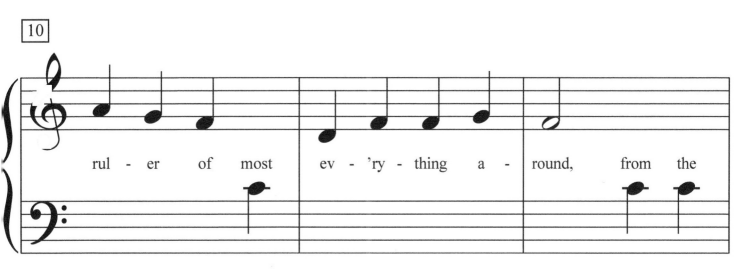

rul - er of most ev - 'ry - thing a - round, from the

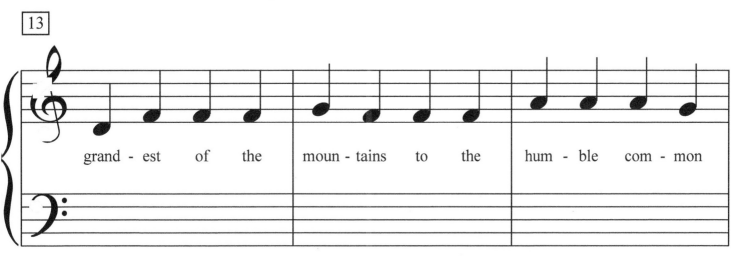

grand - est of the moun - tains to the hum - ble com - mon

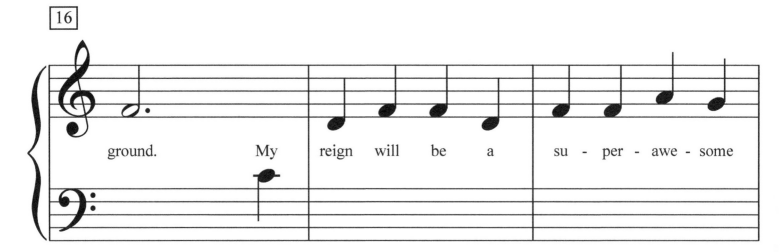

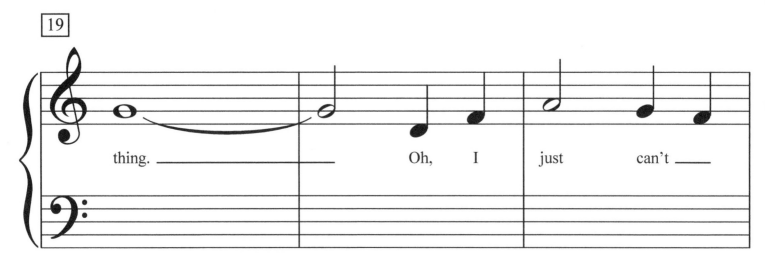

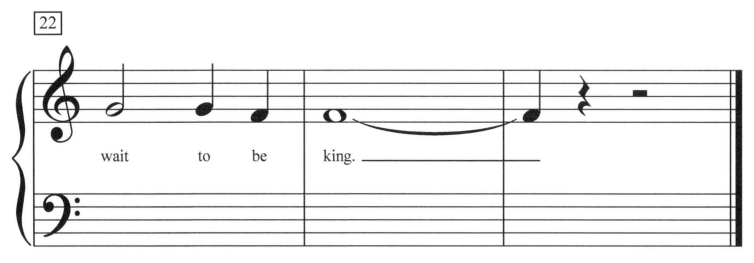

Les Poissons
from Walt Disney's THE LITTLE MERMAID

Music by Alan Menken
Lyrics by Howard Ashman
Arranged by Mona Rejino

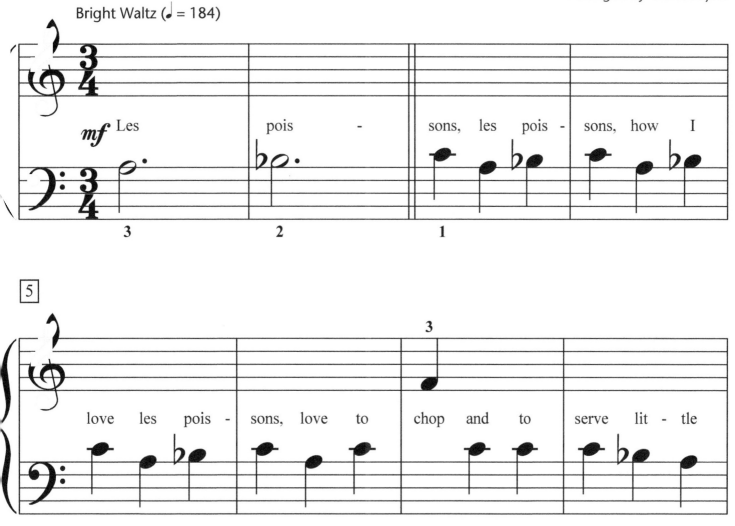

Accompaniment (Student plays one octave higher than written.)

TRACKS 11/12

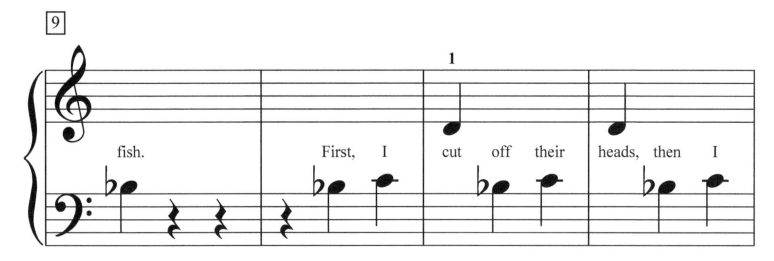

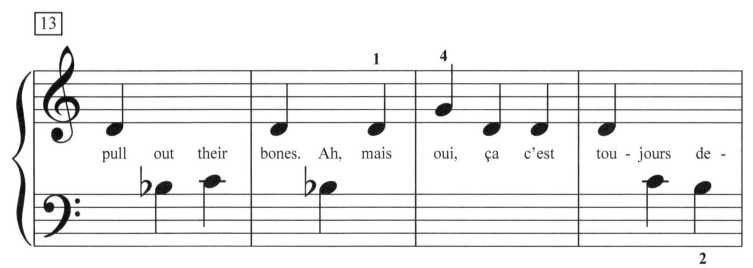

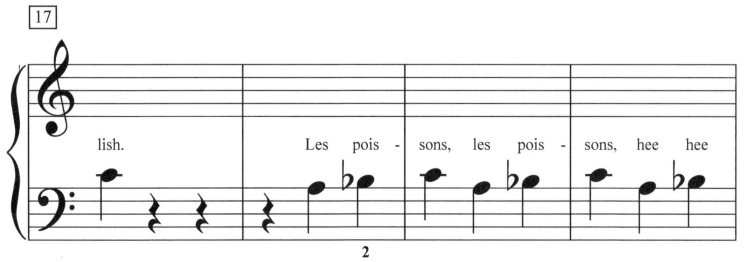

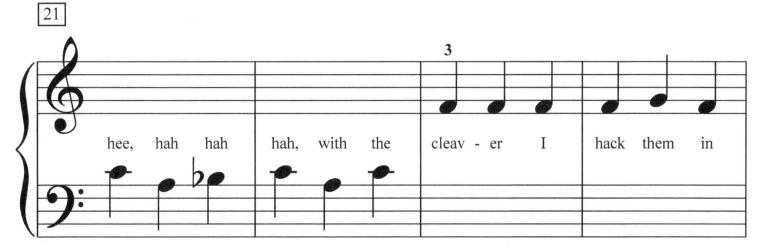

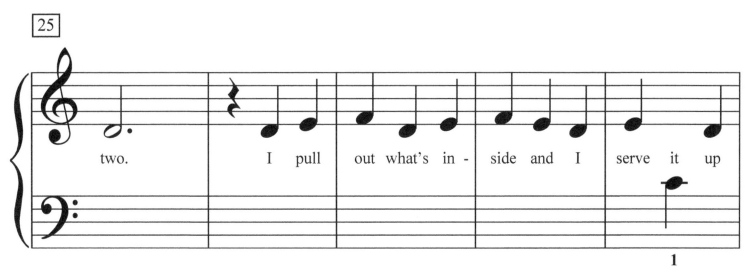

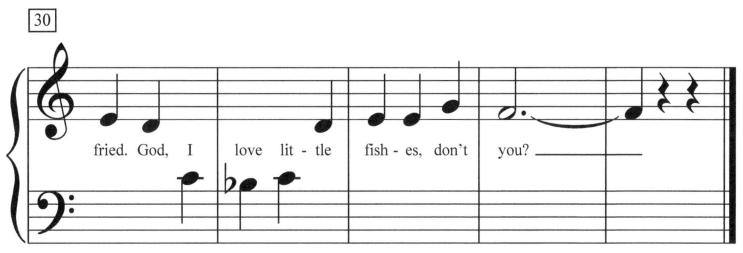

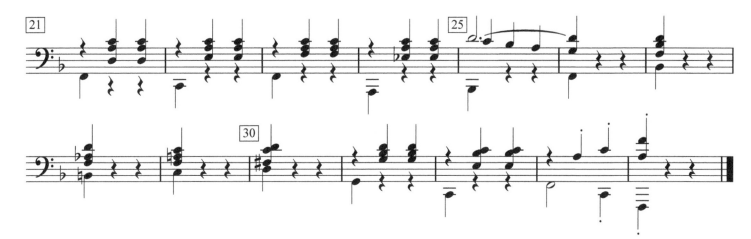

Let's Go Fly a Kite

from Walt Disney's MARY POPPINS

Words and Music by Richard M. Sherman
and Robert B. Sherman
Arranged by Fred Kern

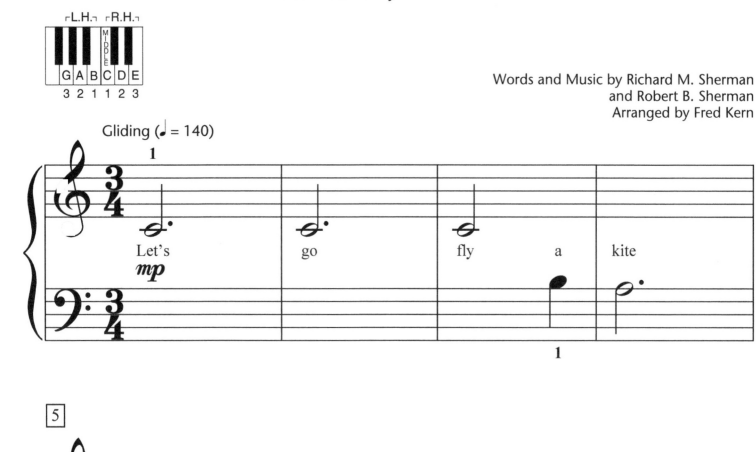

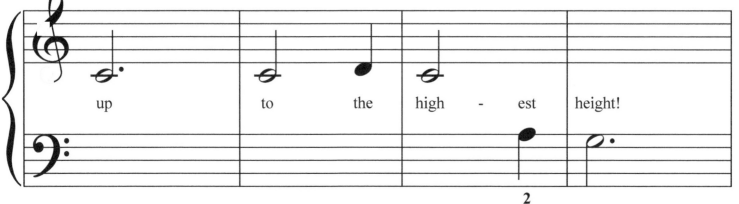

Accompaniment (Student plays one octave higher than written.)

TRACKS 13/14

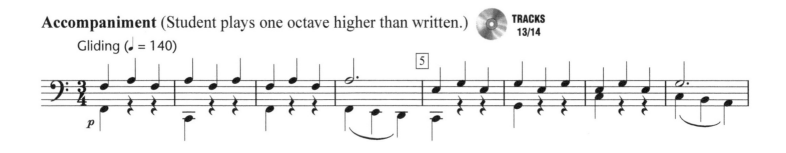

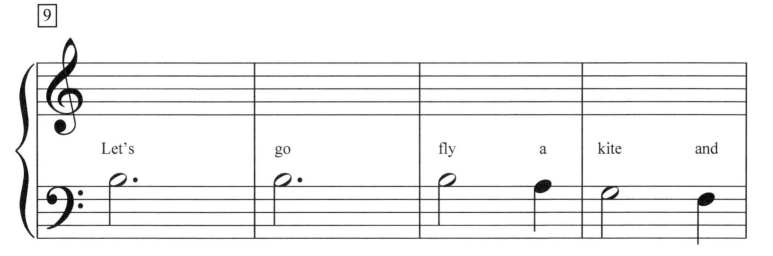

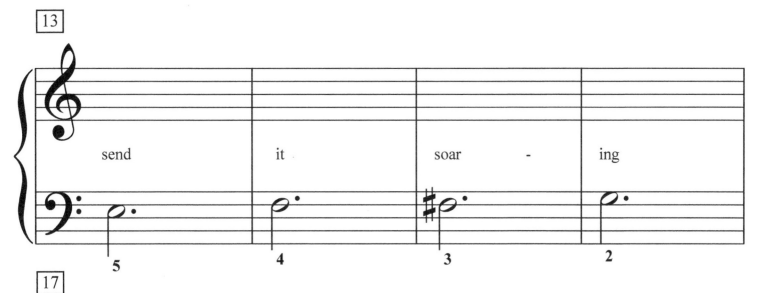

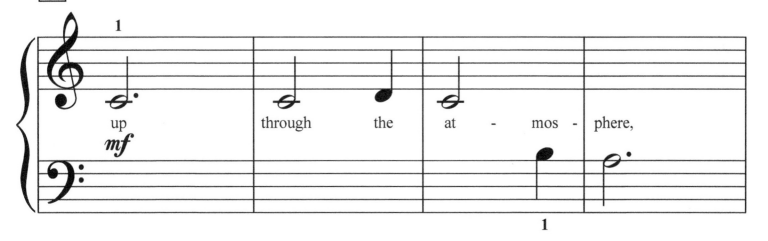

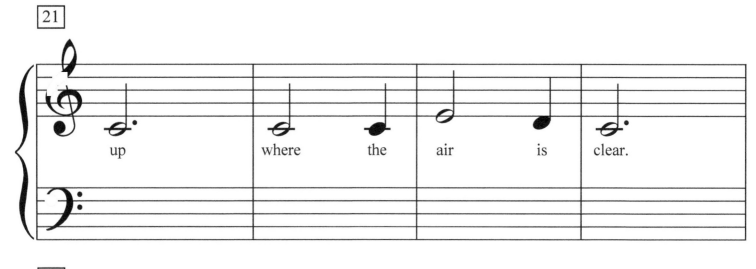

up   where   the   air   is   clear.

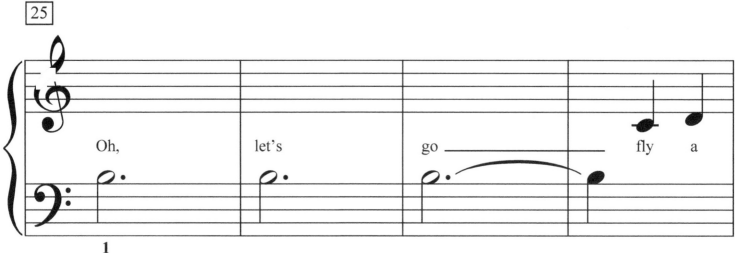

Oh,   let's   go _____ fly   a

1

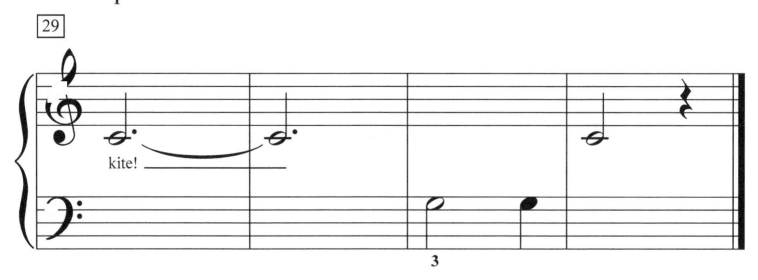

kite! _____

3

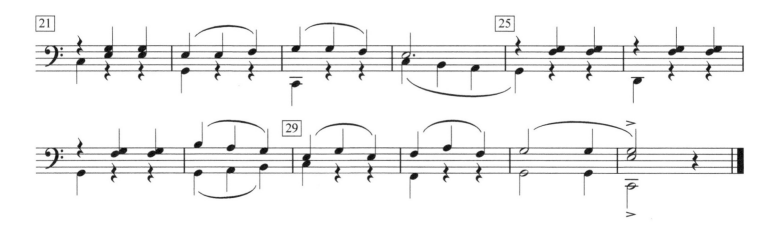

The Music of the Night

from THE PHANTOM OF THE OPERA

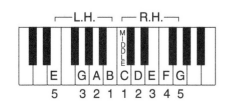

Music by Andrew Lloyd Webber
Lyrics by Charles Hart
Additional Lyrics by Richard Stilgoe
Arranged by Fred Kern

Moderately slow (♩ = 120)

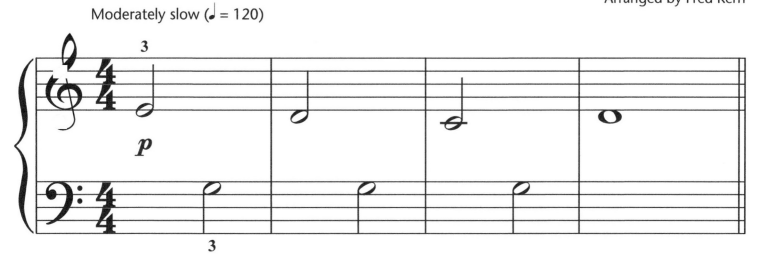

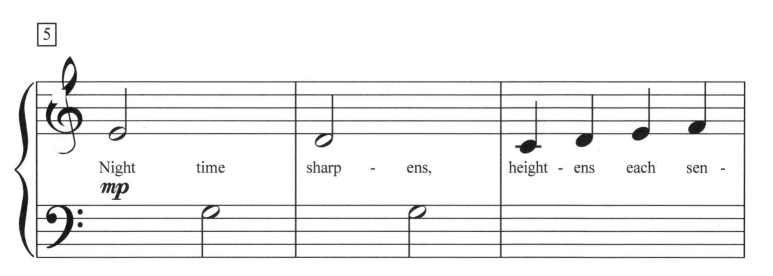

Night time sharp - ens, height - ens each sen -

Accompaniment (Student plays one octave higher than written.) **TRACKS 15/16**

Moderately slow (♩ = 120)

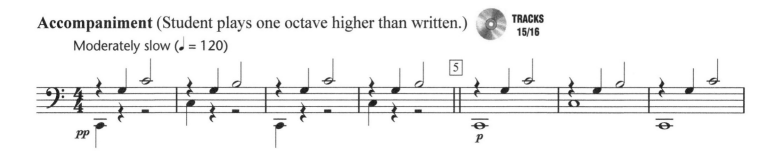

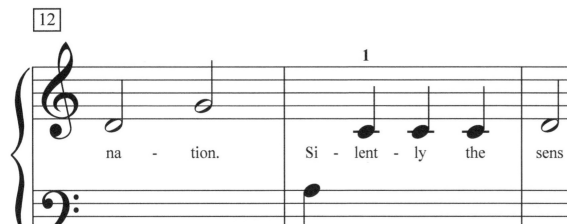

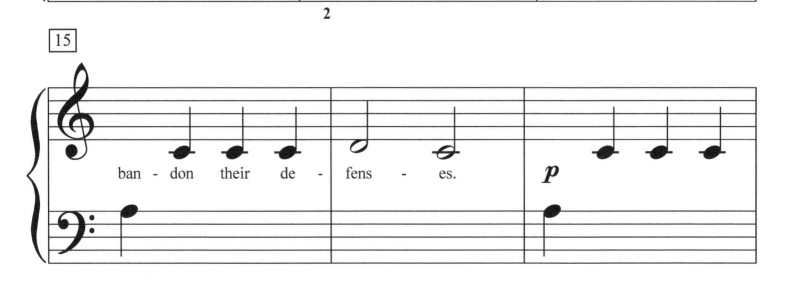

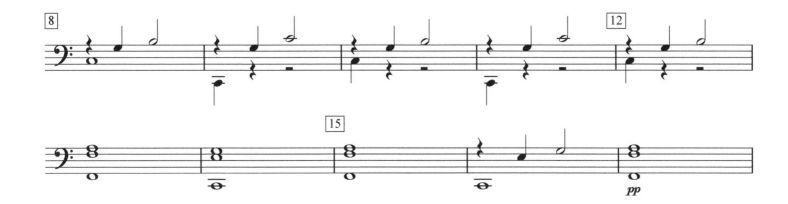

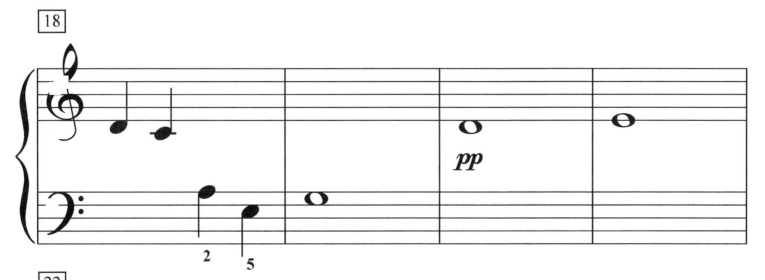

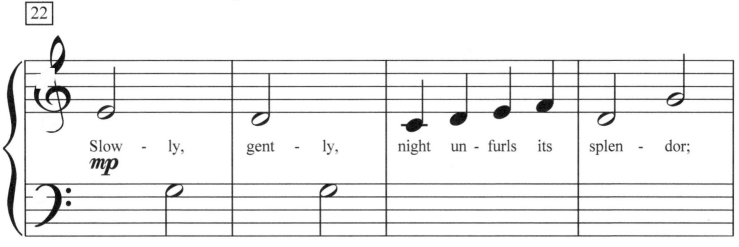

Slow - ly,   gent - ly,   night un - furls its   splen - dor;

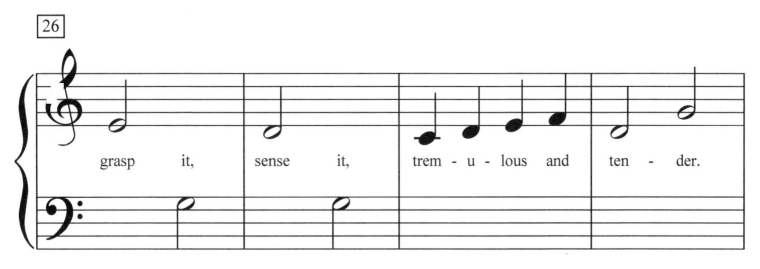

grasp it,   sense it,   trem - u - lous and   ten - der.

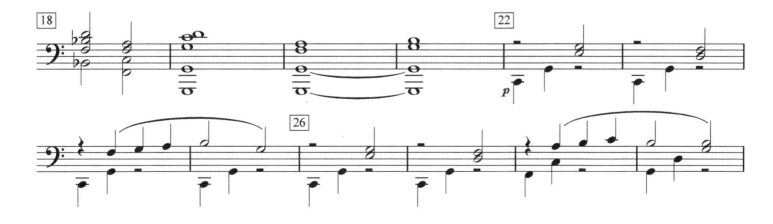

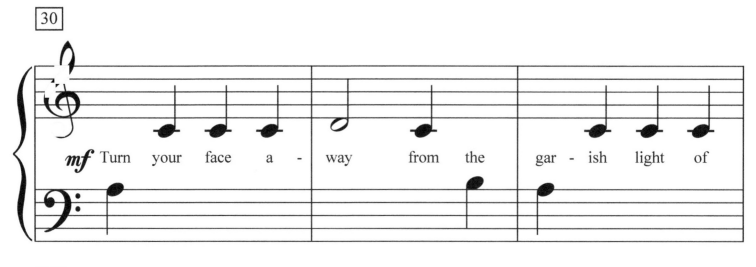

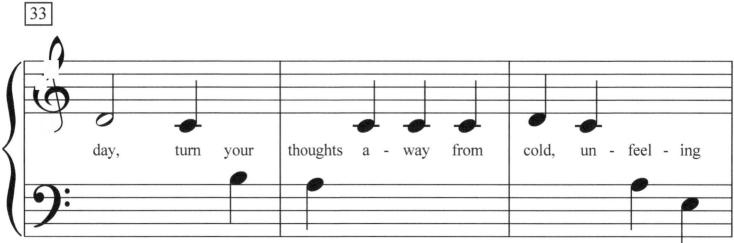

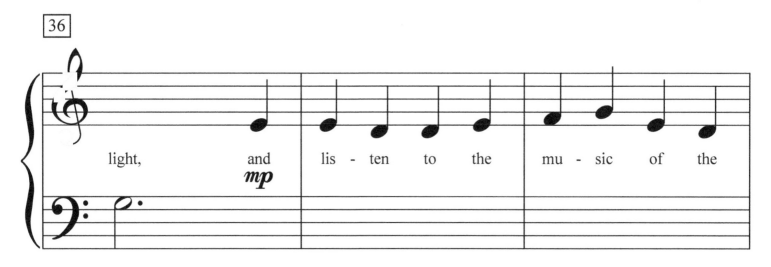

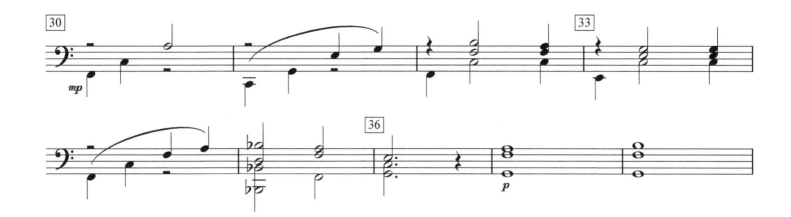

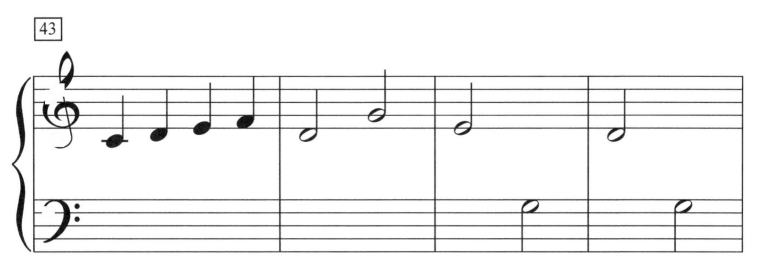

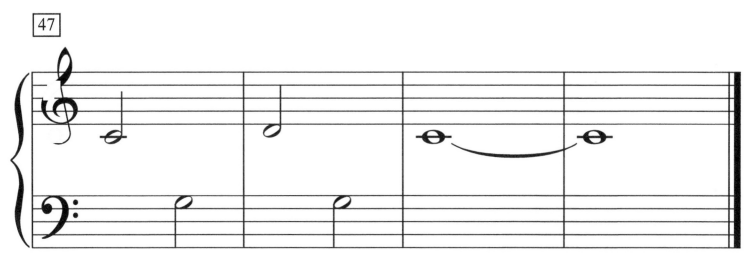

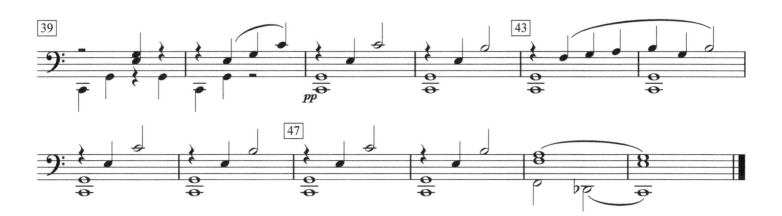

My Heart Will Go On

(Love Theme From 'Titanic')

from the Paramount and Twentieth Century Fox Motion Picture TITANIC

Music by James Horner
Lyric by Will Jennings
Arranged by Mona Rejino

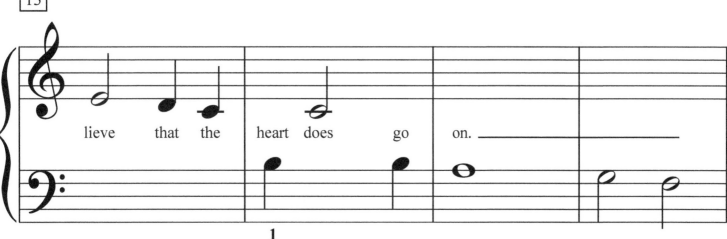

This Is It

Theme from THE BUGS BUNNY SHOW

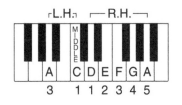

Words and Music by Mack David
and Jerry Livingston
Arranged by Mona Rejino

Lyrics: O - ver - ture, cur - tain, lights, this it it, the night of nights. No

Accompaniment (Student plays one octave higher than written.) TRACKS 19/20

With excitement, in "two" (♩ = 104)

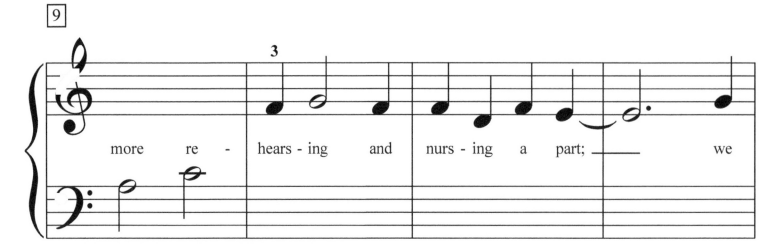

more re - hears - ing and nurs - ing a part; _____ we

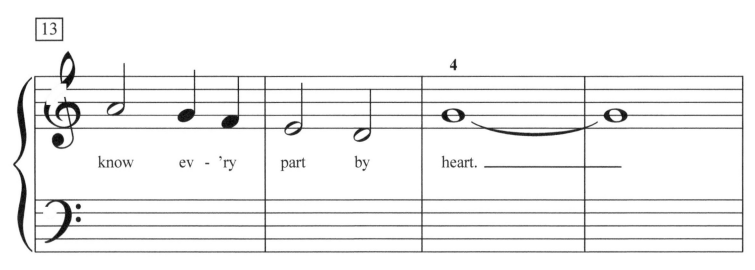

know ev - 'ry part by heart. _____

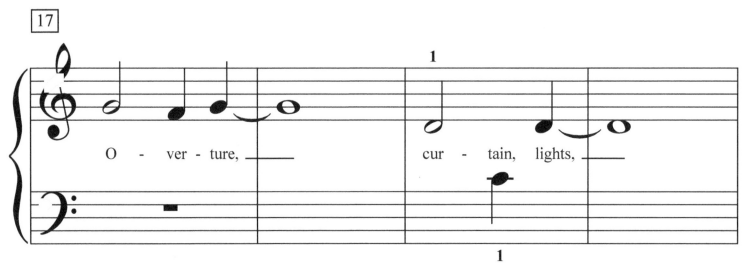

O - ver - ture, _____ cur - tain, lights, _____

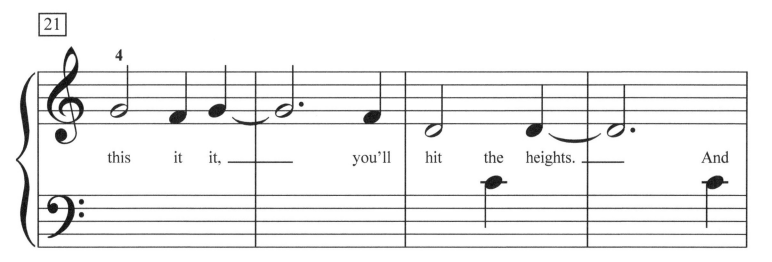

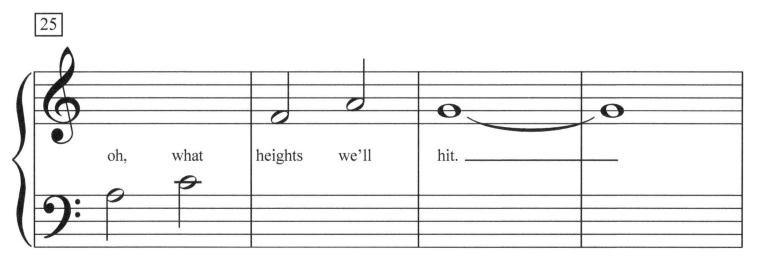

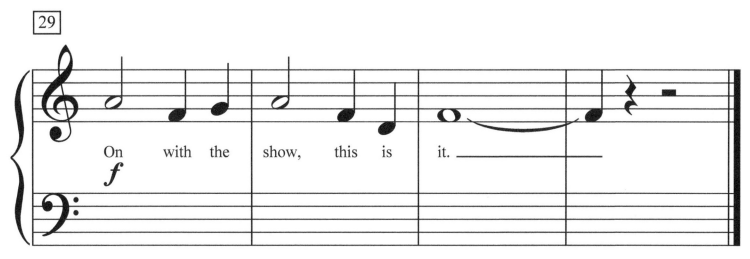

Whistle While You Work

Words by Larry Morey
Music by Frank Churchill

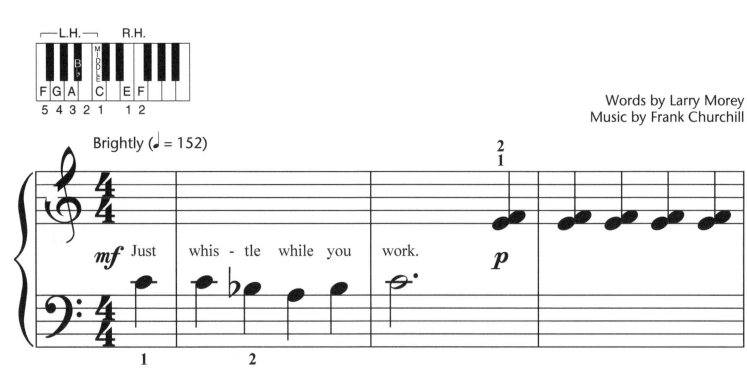

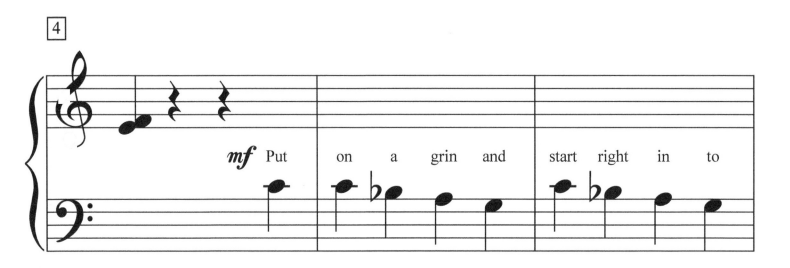

Accompaniment (Student plays one octave higher than written.) **TRACKS 21/22**

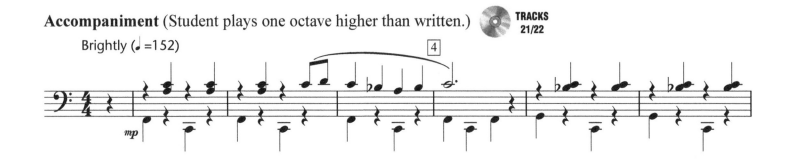

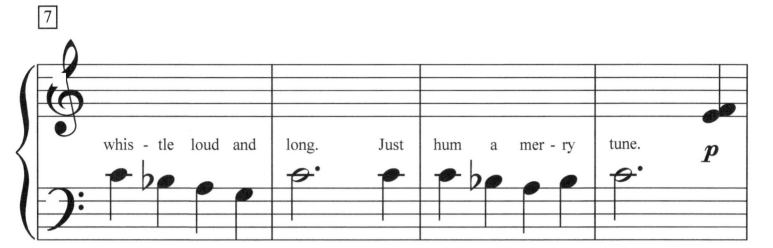

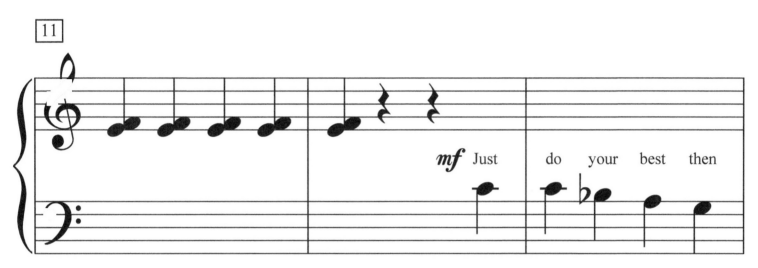

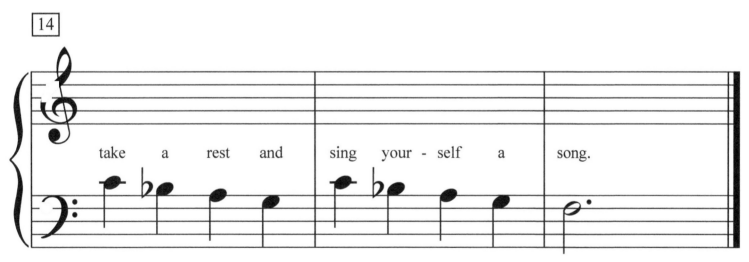

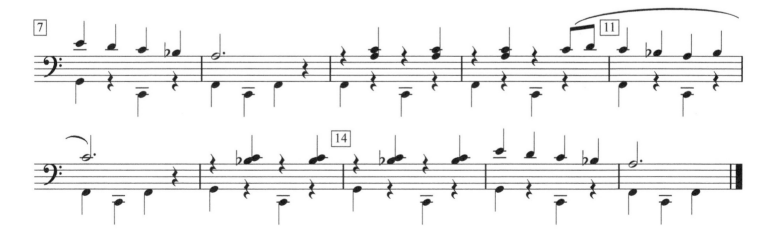

The Wonderful Thing About Tiggers

from Walt Disney's THE MANY ADVENTURES OF WINNIE THE POOH

Words and Music by Richard M. Sherman
and Robert B. Sherman
Arranged by Phillip Keveren

With a bounce (♩. = 76)

mf The won - der - ful

thing a - bout tig - gers _____ is tig - gers are

Accompaniment (Student plays one octave higher than written.) 🔘 **TRACKS 23/24**

With a bounce (♩. = 76)

mp
non legato

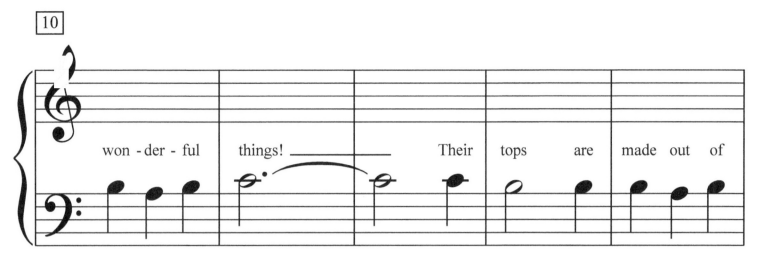

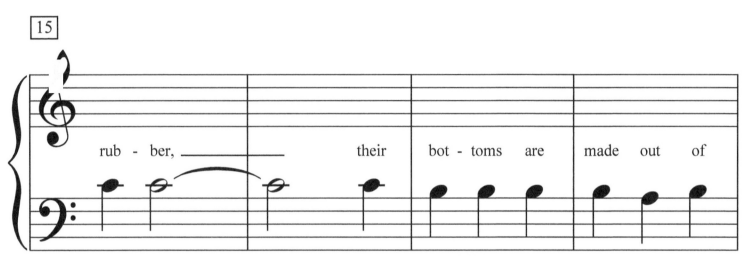

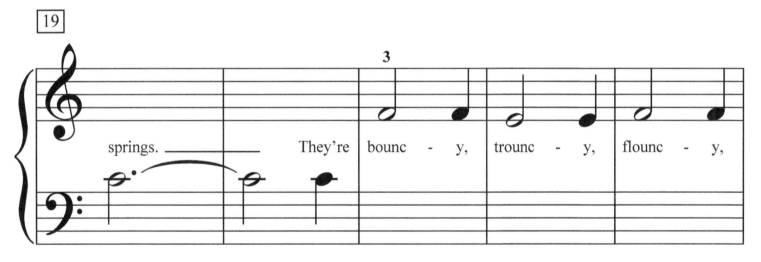

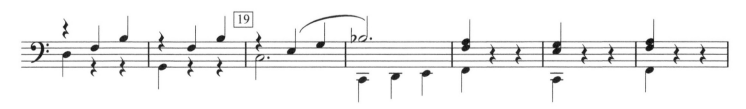

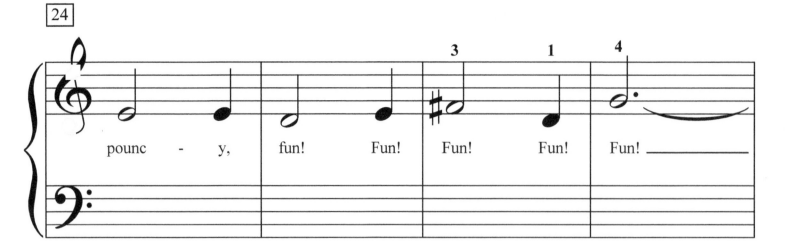

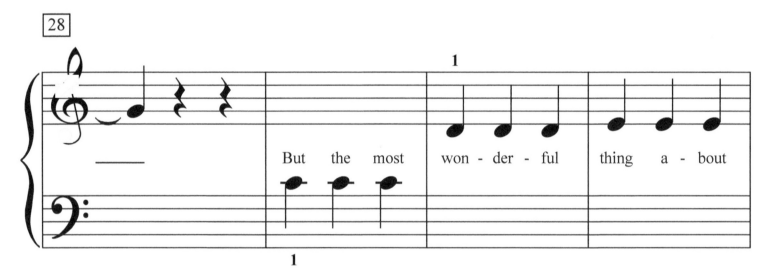

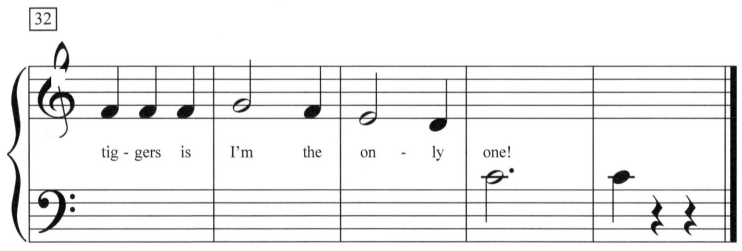